The Symbolism of the Sixty

By

Jeffrey T. Erickson

Jeffrey T. Erickson

ISBN-13:
978-1983882661

ISBN-10:
1983882666

Table of Contents

Table of Contents

Dedication

To anyone who is thinking of "coming back" to Christ.

Acknowledgments

I am grateful to Holly Banks and Marjorie Harris who continue to bless my life through their wonderful editing skills and writing insights.

I am grateful for saints who have courageously returned to the fold of God. I am grateful for enlistments and reenlistments. I am grateful for the remarkable spiritual comebacks of others whom I have been privileged to observe. Much like last-second victories, every return to Christ is incredible to watch and exciting to witness.

I am grateful for the power of the atonement of Jesus Christ in my life. I am grateful to the Lord for the blessing of repentance. I am grateful for the blessing of the Spirit of the Holy Ghost which inspires people to change. I have learned that the Lord is quick to forget, quick to forgive and quick to cleanse. I have learned that no matter how far away we are from Him, He never forgets His children.

I am grateful for the Book of Mormon and the thousands of principles the Lord teaches us through its pages. I am also grateful for the deepened doctrines and greater views which the Spirit shares with me on a daily basis as I study the contents of the greatest book on Earth.

~Jeff

Prologue:

For the past few months our family has been going over to a house we are building and sweeping and cleaning for our Saturday work projects. While this is probably not necessary for the progress of the house, it's a great family project we can do together while teaching the powerful principle of work. We typically take an hour or two to clean and sweep the inside of the unfinished house. My kids continue to tell me it is a pointless task as "the workers" will do it. They are correct in stating that "the workers" will do it, as the goal is to teach them to be "the workers" themselves.

Recently, while at the house sweeping, my nine-year-old daughter Holland wandered off to a different part of the house to escape doing her part. I saw her standing and doing nothing a number of times. I wasn't happy with her work ethic so I asked her a time or two to help out more and get to sweeping. She didn't respond very dutifully. Finally, I reprimanded her and said, "I am not happy with your efforts. I feel you are not helping or working very hard; you need to help more and do better." She was angry with me and stormed off to a different part of the house.

After a short time, I made it to the side of the house where she was now effectively working and sweeping. On her side she had accumulated many piles of dirt, paper, garbage and sawdust. She had been working much harder after the reprimand. She and I finished up together by sweeping up her piles with a dustpan and depositing them into a garbage bag.

On the way home from the house Holland and I had the following discussion. I said, "Holland, I appreciate that you really increased your efforts cleaning after we talked." Young Holland looked at me and proudly and wisely said, "Dad, I finished strong."

This book is about finishing strong, coming back, coming home, converting, cleansing, changing your heart, returning to righteousness, repenting, restoring, returning to activity, restoring faith, realizing wrongs, and righting wrongs through accepting the atonement of Jesus Christ.

I hope this book allows you to realize wherever you have been matters far less than where you are going. I hope you come to see that God's love is endless and timeless, and a loving Father's invitation never expires. I hope you feel the Spirit invite you to come home again and wrap yourself "eternally in the arms of his love" (2 Nephi 1:15). I hope you see the symbolism of the Sixty really means that there is still time to claim the blessings of mercy, which are the richest blessings of eternity. If you learn one lesson from this book, I hope it is "that the gate of heaven is [still] open unto all... who will believe on the name of Jesus

Christ, who is the Son of God" (Helaman 3:28).

The Symbolism of the Sixty

In 2011 the Texas Rangers played the Saint Louis Cardinals in The World Series of Major League Baseball. Entering game six, the Rangers were winning by three games to two. By the bottom of the ninth inning, the Cardinals were down 7-5 with two outs and two strikes on the batter. The Cardinals were literally down to their last strike-- their last chance-- of the series.

For all intents and purposes, the Cardinals were finished; the series would be over in just seconds, and they would soon go down to defeat. Something miraculous happened, though, when they were down to their last strike. There was still a ray of hope. The players were still believing, the fans were still cheering, there was still hope that somehow, and in some way, their team might escape the jaws of defeat..

Then, it happened! As the potential last pitch crossed home plate, the hitter swung mightily. In a desperate last effort, the hitter crushed a double off the right field wall and two runners scored, and the game was suddenly tied. The amazed crowd roared with delight. The game went to extra innings. In the top half of the tenth inning, the Rangers scored two runs to lead 9-7. In the bottom of the tenth, the Cardinals scored one run, but were again down to their last strike of the game. How could this happen yet again? The fans still believed, the players still believed, and--with two outs and two strikes--the batter hit a single to again drive in the tying run. In the second extra inning, the eleventh inning, the Cardinals won game six with a home run and went on to win game seven and the 2011 World Series.

The Cardinals' amazing comeback parallels the spiritual comeback of so many saints' lives. I have seen individuals in many instances--like the Cardinals-- down to their last strike. They are on the edge of defeat when something miraculous happens. Sometimes this pivotal event is a spiritual prompting, an answer to a prayer, a remembrance of something sacred, a temple visit, an inspired friend, a text, a note, a child serving a mission, an old convert, an inspired leader, or a few minutes reading from the pages of the Book of Mormon. Somehow, by the hands of a loving God, they are miraculously rescued from the jaws of defeat. This rescue always comes through the merits of a redeeming Savior who can truly rescue anyone.

I vividly recall a young man in my ward growing up who was never going to go on a mission. During his high school years, he and his friends were "riotous," to use a scriptural term lightly (Luke 15:13). Most of these friends were not of our faith, and their actions further distanced him and them from the faith. I am certain that his family wanted him to go on a mission, but this young man was just not interested in serving the Lord or being a missionary. He really wasn't too interested in being a member of the church. He was having too much worldly fun in his life, and the things of God just weren't important to him. He seemed to be doing exactly the opposite of what Paul said of the faithful: "choosing rather to suffer affliction with the people of God, than to enjoy the pleasures of sin for a season" (Hebrews 11:25).

He was enjoying his season of sin. He loved his rock music, his hair was long, he loved to party, he participated in the vices of the teenage crowd, and his standards were that of a typical, worldly teenager. I am certain that even many of his church leaders had written him off as a troubled teen who was too difficult to have in the ward. He was enjoying the great and spacious building, and his path and course were set--or so he thought. In his mind, nothing was going to stop him from doing what he was doing, and nothing was going to change him. There was, however, one huge obstacle in his path to "the great and spacious building:" his mother (Nephi 8:26). This young man didn't realize how powerful the faith of his mother was. He wasn't aware of the work she was doing behind the scenes to assist him in his life and to redirect his spiritual path.

When his nineteenth birthday rolled around and the reality that her son was not planning to serve a mission hit her, her efforts only increased. She began to fast for her son weekly on Mondays. Her son, already a part of her daily prayers, became the central focus of her daily prayers. I don't know all the details, but I am certain on numerous occasions she desperately pleaded with the Lord just as Alma did for his wayward son. After fasting weekly and increasing the intensity of her prayers for two months, nothing changed. Nothing happened to this young man's actions, disposition, or behavior. This faithful mother never stopped. She continued to fast and fervently pray that her son's heart would change. Over the next few months, her hopes increased as she saw some change of heart, change of countenance, and change of desires. The petitions of her weekly fasts were beginning to bear fruit.

After more than six months of fasting and some spiritual progress, she didn't stop her weekly fasts. She continued with "unshaken faith" and her heartfelt plea's to the Lord (2 Nephi 31:19). A few short weeks later this young man, now approaching twenty, came home one day and said to his mom, "I want to serve a mission." Her faith, her prayers, her devoted fasting, and the faith of others had helped bring about a miracle in this young man's life. He met with a good bishop, confessed, repented, changed, and humbled himself and took all the necessary steps to serve a mission. This repentance process was certainly difficult, but he did everything the bishop asked of him so he could be forgiven and serve a mission with clean hands and a pure heart.

A mother's earnest prayers were answered tenfold as this young man not only served a mission, but was a powerful missionary. He was devoted, loving, hardworking, showed great leadership and had a life changing experience as a missionary. It was easy for me, as a member of his ward, to see the dramatic change in him, his countenance, and his desires when he returned from full-time service.

I will never forget one experience that was shared with me which helped me understand how completely he had turned his life unto the Lord. When he returned home from his missionary service, one of the first phone calls he received was from his old friends. Remember, these were friends that had previously walked with him into "mists of darkness" (Nephi 8:23). His friends called and invited him out with them so it could be just like old times. What a dilemma this young returned missionary faced. He courageously and politely told them that he couldn't go out with them and that things in his life had changed.

I was both amazed and impressed that this young man was able to move on from his past and never look back. He had truly repented, his heart had been changed, and he has not been the same person since. I am aware that he has remained faithful to the Lord to this day, marrying in the temple, raising a wonderful family, and serving faithfully in many capacities in the church.

I am grateful for mothers with faith, I am grateful for mercy, I am grateful for repentance, I am grateful for comebacks, and I am grateful for hearts that change in time, not just on time. I am grateful for the Lord's timetable, which may be quite different and so much more merciful than our own.

I am thrilled to be writing on the topic of hope, mercy and repentance. I am an avid people-watcher and have been for years. As I observe people, I have frequently longed for people who struggle to simply embrace the powerful, mind-altering, life-changing, heart-softening principles of the Saviour. Hope is hard to define and difficult to encapsulate, but when you truly find hope in Christ, it changes everything. Hope is possibly the greatest precursor to faith which is the great precursor to charity. Hope in Christ may be the foundation of the golden tripod of these three Christlike virtues.

Hope may be defined best by what it is not. It is not pessimism, it is not doubt, it is not gloom and doom, it is not negativity, it is not darkness, it is not misery, it is not futility, and it is not faithlessness. Hope is limitless. Hope means with God, anything is possible. Hope is optimism, and hope is anticipation. Hope is possibility and promise. Hope is potential. Hope is that "particle of desire" that Alma speaks of (Alma 32:27). Hope is dreams that come true through Godly intervention. Hope is a confidence in Christ. Hope is courageous. Hope is contagious.

Many years ago, I was working in a downtown area as a dentist. This was a rougher part of town and some of the patients were a little bit rough as well. One day I was working on a patient with Hepatitis B. This is a very contagious disease that can be spread through the saliva or blood. The patient was honest with us about his medical history; therefore we proceeded with all standard precautions.

I finished the emergency dental exam, completed my charting, and left the room. A few minutes later, one of my assistants came up to me with tears in her eyes. She said, "Dr. Erickson, did the patient in room two really have Hepatitis B?" I hesitated as I reviewed where we had been and what we had done. I said, "Yes, he did." Her countenance and heart sunk even deeper. "What happened?" I said.

She told me when she was cleaning the room that she had accidentally been stuck by a dental instrument, the explorer, on the dental tray. For a moment, my heart sunk for her. She and I both knew this meant the possibility of contracting Hepatitis B, which in many ways has a life sentence similar to HIV. I thought for a moment remembering something significant and looked at her and said, "When I did the exam I never used the dental explorer." I could see a dramatic shift in her face, and her eyes lit up again with joy and happiness. I saw hope return to her countenance in a dramatic fashion. She was thrilled with the news.

This book is written for people that need a little bit more hope. For those that may be in need of a comeback, a restoration of faith, and a return of optimism, this book is for you. I would like to begin with one of my favorite Book of Mormon stories found in Alma, the stripling warriors, followed by a little scriptural liberty that will hopefully bless someone in need of hope and light. This story begins in Alma chapter 53 verse 10:

And now behold, I have somewhat to say concerning the people of Ammon, who, in the beginning, were Lamanites; but by Ammon and his brethren, or rather by the power and word of God, they had been converted unto the Lord; and they had been brought down into the land of Zarahemla, and had ever since been protected by the Nephites.

And because of their oath they had been kept from taking up arms against their brethren; for they had taken an oath that they never would shed blood more; and according to their oath they would have perished; yea, they would have suffered themselves to have fallen into the hands of their brethren, had it not been for the pity and the exceeding love which Ammon and his brethren had had for them.

And for this cause they were brought down into the land of Zarahemla; and they ever had been protected by the Nephites.

But it came to pass that when they saw the danger, and the many afflictions and tribulations which the Nephites bore for them, they were moved with compassion and were desirous to take up arms in the defense of their country.

But behold, as they were about to take their weapons of war, they were overpowered by the persuasions of Helaman and his brethren, for they were about to break the oath which they had made.

And Helaman feared lest by so doing they should lose their souls; therefore, all those who had entered into this covenant were compelled to behold their brethren wade through their afflictions, in their dangerous circumstances at this time.

But behold, it came to pass they had many sons, who had not entered into a covenant that they would not take their weapons of war to defend themselves against their enemies; therefore, they did assemble themselves together at this time, as many as were able to take up arms, and they called themselves Nephites.

And they entered into a covenant to fight for the liberty of the Nephites, yea, to protect the land unto the laying down of their lives; yea, even they covenanted that they never would give up their liberty, but they would fight in all cases to protect the Nephites and themselves from bondage.

Now behold, there were two thousand of those young men, who entered into this covenant and took their weapons of war to defend their country.

And now behold, as they never had hitherto been a disadvantage to the Nephites, they became now at this period of time also a great support; for they took their weapons of war, and they would that Helaman should be their leader.

And they were all young men, and they were exceedingly valiant for courage, and also for strength and activity; but behold, this was not all—they were men who were true at all times in whatsoever thing they were entrusted.

Yea, they were men of truth and soberness, for they had been taught to keep the commandments of God and to walk uprightly before him (Alma 53:10-21).

When Helaman took charge of the 2000 stripling warriors, they went to battle filled with faith, and the Lord rewarded their efforts in miraculous ways. The experiences of the stripling warriors are truly some of the most astonishing and remarkable experiences in all of scripture. There is no earthly way the things that happened to them could have happened to them without the hand of God miraculously directing, protecting and defending them.

Have you ever wondered what happened to the young men who were anti-Nephi-Lehi's who stayed home? Have you ever wondered if some stayed home because they weren't ready yet? Have you ever wondered if some stayed home because they weren't qualified? Have you ever wondered if some stayed home because they didn't feel worthy? Have you ever wondered if some were just afraid to make the commitment to go? Have you ever wondered if some just didn't have the same testimony that the 2000 had? Have you ever wondered if some thought it just wasn't the right time to fight? Have you ever thought maybe some hadn't prepared well enough to be called into the service? Have you ever thought that maybe some thought they would just go to battle at a later time? Have you ever thought that some just were not interested in serving in the military at the time? Have you ever wondered if a few of them thought it wasn't a great idea to fight the Lamanites altogether?

I would like to use a little scriptural liberty to sufficiently answer these questions for myself. Here is what I am certain of: not every young man went to battle with Helaman. Not every young man was prepared to go on the day when the first battalion of two thousand volunteered to serve. Every young man that didn't go missed out on incredible experiences that were life-changing. They missed out on some of the most miraculous events in history. They missed out on seeing the Lord's hand protect 2000 young men in a never-before-seen manner. They missed out on some significant life-altering experiences. They missed out on some things so sacred that most details were not even recorded for us. They missed some miraculous events, but mercy--as it always is--was still granted to those who went later.

For the people who didn't enlist early, one decision did not dictate their destiny; there was still time to make good decisions. There was still time to serve. There was still time to change, to repent, and to accept a call to serve. They had missed a wonderful opportunity, but it was not too late to seize other meaningful opportunities.

All of this leads me to a pressing question: why did Helaman, Mormon and Captain Moroni spend time writing about the sixty young men who enlisted later? In Alma chapter 57 verse 6 we read that *"sixty of the sons of the Ammonites... had come to join their brethren."*

In all of scripture, we see unique numbers; we frequently see the importance of the one, and we often see certain numbers like three, seven and twelve. These numbers are significant. In all of scripture, there is only one time that the precise number of sixty is mentioned. I find it both intriguing and fascinating the Lord would have the prophets take the time to write of sixty isolated young men, when there were already thousands and literally tens of thousands serving for the Nephites in the military. When the sixty arrived to support Helaman, there were 6,000 others arriving with them, but those 6,000 are never spoken of in detail. There is a possibility that all 60 of those young men could have joined sooner, but they didn't. It is of note that they didn't enlist initially, but more importantly, that they did eventually engage and enlist.

Let me share one possible explanation as to why Helaman spoke with meticulous precision about the sixty. I want to call this the "Symbolism of the Sixty." For me, "the Sixty" are a constant reminder that when we miss an opportunity, it is not the end. The Sixty are a reminder that when mistakes are made, sins of omission or commission are committed, we haven't defaulted our spiritual standing permanently. The Sixty are a symbol of second chances. The Sixty are an example that it is better to enlist, embark, and engage late than not at all. The Sixty show that repentance still brings about incredible blessings. The Sixty are a symbol that repentance at any time still brings a purity of spirit and body. The Sixty send a message that opportunities missed or lost can be restored. The Sixty will forever be a sign that repentance rightfully restores. Repentance restores blessings, faith, hope, sacred experiences, priesthood, power, relationships, opportunity, losses, the Spirit, and the gift of eternal life. The Sixty could be a precious reminder to every one of us that we don't always do things right the first time; we procrastinate, we neglect, we postpone, we reject opportunity, we defer blessings, we delay growth, we sin, we turn away from God, we fall short, and we make some awful decisions. But God will not allow us to be defined by poor decisions.

One of the greatest achievement awards I have ever heard about is called the "Red Lantern Award." The Award has been given out every year at the Iditarod Dog race since 1993. The Iditarod sled dog race is a nearly 1000 mile race that is usually run from Willow to Nome, Alaska. The race is often appropriately referred to as the last great race on earth. The race is run by a team of 16 dogs and a musher in the harshest of conditions, such as blizzards causing whiteout conditions, sub-zero temperatures and gale force winds, and wind chills up to -100 Fahrenheit. The Iditarod trail is approximately 975-1000 miles, depending on the course they choose, and consists of a variety of terrains such as forests, hills, tundra, mountain passes, and even across rivers. This race is not for the faint of heart.

The Red Lantern award is not given for placing first, for winning, or for being in one of the top dog sled teams. Racers competing in the Iditarod race know the Red Lantern award is a symbol of perseverance. The award is given every year not to the person who finishes the Iditarod first, but who finishes the race dead last. The award is given to someone who finishes last in the race, but never gives up and never quits the race. The Red Lantern award truly is an award for competing, persisting, enduring, and finishing.

I have come to this conclusion in life: God gives out millions of Red Lantern awards for those who fall short but never quit and finish the race of life. I have also concluded that one of the things God may love most about being God is giving out Red Lantern awards.

In many states there is a "Tough Mudder" event. In this event people usually compete in groups and they run either five or ten miles. During the running there is different obstacles you encounter that deal with mud. Last year a few of our family competed in the event. I learned one powerful lesson from the event that was repeated over and over again. They constantly reminded the participants; this is a "team competition" not a race. Their message was powerful as the event was never about winning, rather about finishing and helping others to finish. I am certain that the Lord would more appropriately like life to be called a team competition rather than a race. The plan of salvation will never be about finishing first, but will always be about just finishing.

One of the deepest, most merciful doctrines the Savior taught was given in a brief, yet illuminating discussion with Peter: *"Then came Peter to him, and said, Lord, how oft shall my brother sin against me, and I forgive him? till seven times? Jesus saith unto him, I say not unto thee, Until seven times: but, Until seventy times seven."* (Matthew 18:21-22

I have watched the Lord mercifully forgive in my own life and the lives of others seventy times seven.

The scriptures remind us that, "To every thing there is a season, and a time to every purpose under the heaven" (Ecclesiastes 3:1).

The Sixty are a reminder that there is a time to forgive. The Lord said, "I, the Lord, will forgive whom I will forgive" (D&C 64:10).

I have also learned that the Lord will forgive *when* He will forgive. When He forgives is a beautiful principle of timing, as sometimes His "when" is far different from when we or others would forgive.

The principle of the Sixty is not an attempt to excuse disobedience, to support premeditated sin, or to say the cost of transgression is not substantial and consequential. The principle of the Sixty is to teach that true and sincere repentance absolutely cleanses. Earnest repentance is one of the greatest necessities of life. Without heartfelt repentance we can never change our character and never truly become children of Christ. True repentance will always be a part of qualifying for the Spirit, qualifying for forgiveness, qualifying for cleanliness, and qualifying for eternal life. I hope this book stands as a witness of the necessity of repentance no matter what the cost or when the time for those who desire to "partake of the goodness of God" (Jacob 1:7).

In the church, people sometimes come back into activity later, we sometimes serve later, we sometimes go on missions later. We sometimes get our temple blessings later than we could have. We sometimes don't get sealed until a later date. We sometimes linger as a prospective elder. We sometimes get distracted for one reason or another and quit living some of the gospel principles. The key to the gospel of Jesus Christ will never be where we have been in the past, but rather, where we are and what we are doing now. A loving Savior mercifully preserves blessings for those who come late to the Savior's table.

One of my favorite parables of the New Testament is that of the two sons in the 21st chapter of Matthew: *But what think ye? A certain man had two sons; and he came to the first, and said, Son, go work today in my vineyard. He answered and said, I will not: but afterward he repented, and went. And he came to the second, and said likewise. And he answered and said, I go, sir: and went not.*

Whether of them twain did the will of his father? They say unto him, The first. Jesus saith unto them, Verily I say unto you, That the publicans and the harlots go into the kingdom of God before you. For John came unto you in the way of righteousness, and ye believed him not: but the publicans and the harlots believed him: and ye, when ye had seen it, repented not afterward, that ye might believe him (Matthew 21:28-32).

Like the first son, there are times when we sin, we break covenants, we reject the promptings of God, or we fail to do that which God would have us do. God knew we would do this so He provided a Savior and numerous second chances through the Atonement of Jesus Christ. There is power in "repenting afterward." There is power in waking up and realizing we were on the wrong path. There is power in the realignment of our priorities. There is power in "changing our hearts" (Mosiah 5:2). There is power in forgiveness.

There is a time to repent, to go back, to make right, to decide again, to change, to turn from, to return, to apply the atonement of

Jesus Christ through second chances, and that time is now; "And thus we see, that there was a time granted unto man to repent, yea, a probationary time, a time to repent and serve God" (Alma 42:4).

It is imperative that we as saints remember that people still have time. We often conclude when people make bad decisions that their probationary time is up, but it is not. There are instances where we need to allow time, "wait on the Lord," pray, plead, fast and endure (Psalm 27:14).

It is in these instances when true mercy is required by patient saints.

A few years ago, a thirteen-year-old girl came to our dental office with a speech impediment. She could speak satisfactorily, but she slurred some sounds and there were certain letters she could not enunciate clearly. Her speech had sounded the same her entire life, and it wasn't nearly as good as it could have been. We discovered the cause of her speech impairment was due to her being tongue tied. The muscle below her tongue was so taut that she could not enunciate certain sounds as clearly as she should have been able to.

For years she had been unsatisfied with her speech but had done nothing about it. After years of self-consciousness and being constantly embarrassed by her speech, we performed a small and simple procedure of cutting or detaching the muscle. This simple surgery allowed her tongue to move much more freely. The procedure took less than ten minutes and was covered by her insurance carrier. She returned to the dental office the following week extremely happy. She called her new speech "terrific," and she felt her English was much better and much clearer now.

What if she had never come in to be evaluated? What if she never would have had this procedure performed on her tongue? She could have come in years earlier, but she didn't. She and her parents waited, and I am not certain why. But what's most important is she finally came in to have her speech altered and improved. She was finally able to make necessary corrections, and it transformed her speech into normal, clear tones. It took her much longer than it should have, but in the end, the decision to come in was an absolute blessing in her life. She had delayed, but now she is delighted with her decision.

Years ago, I taught a lesson in Gospel Doctrine class and I wrote out a $1,000,000 check to the class. I showed the check to the class and told them the check would be good so it could be cashed. "The only problem," I said, "is that I will make the check good in time. The time the check can be cashed is 100 years from the date of the lesson." This is the true lesson of the Sixty. God's promises are good for all of us. Some of us lay claim on the blessings early, some late, and some after darkness, but the most important thing we can do is make certain that we accept the check. We must never begrudge others for not cashing the Lord's check early. For some, it takes a while to recognize the value of the gift or even to believe the gift is real. Whether the Lord's check is cashed now or later, it still will be of great worth when it is tendered.

Jeffrey T. Erickson

I witnessed some of the Sixty in my mission as a full-time missionary. I remember two Elders, one who was twenty-six years old and the other who was twenty-seven years old. It was obvious that both of these good brothers didn't enlist when the other "2000" local missionaries did at nineteen years of age. They enlisted a few years later, but I am certain they were grateful for a second chance. Their second chance still provided them the opportunity to join the Lord's team of missionaries when they did. I am certain they were glad the war with the adversary was still going and that--even though it was late-- it was not too late to enlist for service. These two brothers went out and served faithfully and were blessed with wonderful mission experiences.

It would never have been appropriate to ask these two powerful Elders, "why did you come into the field so late?" Why would any missionary ever begrudge another Elder or Sister for coming out later to serve with them on the Lord's team? The only appropriate thought for these two these faithful Elders would be, "What a blessing that you came to serve in God's army." Serving with the two of them was not only a privilege, but a lesson I pray I will never forget. Through these two stripling warriors, I was again reminded we believe in a God of mercy, a God of forgiveness, and a God of second chances.

A few months ago my fifteen-year-old son Talmage was preparing to iron a shirt. He has been around an iron plenty in his lifetime. He knows that irons are extremely hot and they will sear your skin. He knows you are not supposed to touch the iron when it is turned on or you will get burned. Talmage stared at the iron waiting for a minute or two for it to get hotter, so he could iron his shirt. He then reached out with his index finger and put it up against the heated metal for about a full second. This was not your split-second touch, but a prolonged touch. It burned his index finger and he was in pain. I quickly said, "Why did you do that?" I don't think my response was helpful. I believe he realized he had just done something dumb. I know he immediately regretted what he had done. He didn't need someone to remind him of his poor decision; he needed someone to tend to his finger.

I believe the Sixty are like Talmage. They are aware of their decisions. They have regret, remorse, and even they wonder at times why they did what they did. They don't need people to remind them of their poor decisions or of their past or condemn them for their sins. They need people who have mercy and who want to help them heal. The Lord said,

> *For the kingdom of heaven is like unto a man that is an householder, which went out early in the morning to hire labourers into his vineyard. And when he had agreed with the labourers for a penny a day, he sent them into his vineyard. And he went out about the third hour, and saw others standing idle in the marketplace, and said unto them; Go ye also into the vineyard, and whatsoever is right, I will give you. And they went their way. Again he went out about the sixth and ninth hour, and did likewise. And about the eleventh hour he went out, and found others standing idle, and saith unto them, Why stand ye here all the day idle? They say unto him,*

because no man hath hired us. He saith unto them, go ye also into the vineyard; and whatsoever is right, that shall ye receive. So when even was come, the lord of the vineyard saith unto his steward, Call the labourers, and give them their hire, beginning from the last unto the first. And when they came that were hired about the eleventh hour, they received every man a penny. But when the first came, they supposed that they should have received more; and they likewise received every man a penny. And when they had received it, they murmured against the good man of the house, Saying, these last have wrought but one hour, and thou hast made them equal unto us, which have borne the burden and heat of the day. But he answered one of them, and said, Friend, I do thee no wrong: didst not thou agree with me for a penny? Take that thine is, and go thy way: I will give unto this last, even as unto thee. Is it not lawful for me to do what I will with mine own? Is thine eye evil, because I am good?" (Matthew 20:1-15).

In the parable of the Laborer in the Vineyard, there are numerous valuable principles taught. One lesson from the laborers who were found during the third hour, the sixth hour, the ninth hour, and even the eleventh hour is that they are representatives of the Sixty. Some of the Sixty come into the Lord's vineyard early and some come later. A second lesson found in this parable is that it would be tragic for someone entering the vineyard during the ninth hour to be upset with someone coming in during the eleventh hour. Thirdly, there are significant rewards and blessings that come while working in the vineyard that are not part of the pay at the end of the day. Fourth, the Lord has assured every laborer that we will receive whatsoever is right." Fifth, I would surmise that nearly all of us at some point stand "idle in the marketplace."

In life and in the church, there are individuals who don't labor early or who start later than they should have started. The Saviour powerfully teaches through this parable that it is not when you start your labors that matters, but that you are willing to accept the invitation to finish your labors. In many ways, He simply reminds us, "but one hour." It will never be how long you labor, but will always be about being willing to labor. This parable also masterfully reminds us that God is merciful and His mercy is far reaching. We also learn that whoever accepts and acts on the Lord's invitation is paid the goodly wage. President Hinckley shared this story:

> [One] morning in stake conference, the president with whom I had stayed was released after thirteen years of faithful service. There was a great outpouring of love and appreciation, not because of his wealth, not because of his stature in the business community, but because of the great service he had unselfishly given. Without thought of personal interest, he had driven tens of thousands of miles in all kinds of weather. He had spent literally thousands of hours in the interest of others. He had neglected his personal affairs to assist those who needed his help. And in so doing he had

come alive and had become great in the eyes of those he had served.

A new president was installed that morning, and there were many who were proud and happy concerning him; but most proud and most happy was a man who sat at the stake clerk's table, a rural mail carrier by profession. He it was who, twelve years ago, had with quiet, patient labor persuaded his totally inactive neighbor to come back into activity.

It would have been so much easier to have let that indifferent neighbor go his own way, and it would have been so much easier for the mail carrier to have lived his own quiet life. But he had put aside his personal interests in the interest of another; and that other person became that Sunday the honored and respected leader of a great stake of Zion. As the people sustained their new president, the man at the clerk's table wept tears of gratitude. In living beyond himself, he had brought to life the man sustained that morning as stake president" (Gordon B. Hinckley, "Whosoever Will Save His Life" Ensign, August 1982, p. 3.).

I am certain the members of that stake were grateful for a man who re-enlisted in the Lord's cause so he could reap the blessings of the Sixty. I am certain this newly called stake president was grateful for the opportunity to come and labor during this ninth or eleventh hour of his life.

I recently had a wonderful man in my ward remind me that he hadn't served a mission as a young man. He reminded me he was in good company with President Monson, President Uchtdorff and a few other prominent church leaders. He wasn't seeking to make excuses; he was merely acknowledging there are great people who have missed out on the opportunity of a mission in their youth. In my mind, his words were a reminder that a loving God didn't limit the blessings to these people, but He kept blessing them and causing them to feel His love in their lives.

The man who reminded me of these great leaders struggled when he was young, but returned to church activity with an assertiveness and faithfulness that has blessed numerous lives. He married a wonderful woman, and they have been sealed and have had many sons and a daughter. Their sons have served full-time missions and all of their children but one has married in the temple. I have seen him employ numerous young people from the church over the years, even myself. He has served faithfully and diligently in many callings and he and his good wife continue to bless many lives in profound ways through their faithfulness. Yes, he missed some early opportunities, but he has had a remarkable comeback since those early long-forgotten times. The Lord didn't quit on him, and like many other wonderful church members, I have watched as a God of mercy has blessed him tenfold for things he may have missed when he wasn't serving God.

In our lives, I am certain that all of us as members of the Sixty have somehow justified our decisions or rationalized our actions which have kept or led us away for a season. The excuses may be varied, and in some cases the excuses may even appear legitimate. The reasons for "standing idle" in the marketplace may range from simple to complex: casualness, disinterest, cares of the world, tithing, neglect, wealth, power, position, pride, being offended, a doctrine, a leader, a disagreement, a divorce, a loss of trust, loss of a loved one, adversity, hidden sins, or any number of other frustrations with the church of Christ. No matter the explanation or excuse, there is no justification worthy of rejecting the blessings and love of God that come to those who desire to "feast upon his love" (Jacob 3:2).

The symbolism of the Sixty helps us understand that a loving God knows that sometimes we are not prepared when called the first time or the second time. The symbolism of the Sixty is that a merciful God understands that we fall short, we sin, we fail, we are distracted, we are unprepared, our faith is weak, but He doesn't quit on us. Nephi powerfully reminded us of the Sixty when he saw our day and said, "For notwithstanding I shall lengthen out mine arm unto them from day to day, they will deny me; nevertheless, I will be merciful unto them, saith the Lord God, if they will repent and come unto me; for mine arm is lengthened out all the day long, saith the Lord God of Hosts" (2 Nephi 28:32).

I love that even when we disappoint Him by our decisions, God still reaches out to us in a merciful way.

A few years ago, I was sitting in sacrament meeting when in walked one-year-old Stella Skinner. She was a beautiful little blonde girl whose father was the executive secretary of the ward. He had left early for meetings that Sunday and so she had not seen him since the day before. She walked in and saw him and her beautiful little eyes lit up. She then very loudly (she hadn't learned chapel reverence yet) and excitedly said, "Da, Da." She then ran to him and they threw their arms around each other.

When we have distanced ourselves from God, but finally come to see Him again, I believe the reunion is similar. I have frequently observed Heavenly Father quickly throw His loving arms around His children to comfort, bless, protect, sustain, invite and welcome them back.

The lesson of the Sixty is that God does not continue to punish us for the past, but that He is ready to forget, forgive, move on and bless us with the future in mind. Think of those who have been prospective Elders for years before finally receiving the higher priesthood. The priesthood blessings they offer are equally as powerful as that of a long-standing Elder.

The grateful greeting to those who have delayed their return, but have finally anxiously returned should never be, "Where have you been or why did you come so late?" The declaration of introduction to these greatly missed and critically needed warriors should always be a forward looking thought. We should enthusiastically echo the words of a loving God who might say, "I am glad you are here. I needed you, I missed you, I love you, I forgive you; now watch what I can do with you."

Elder Donald L. Hallstrom said, "Well, we meet in this priesthood meeting because who we are, is not who we can become" (2014 April GC "What manner of men?). The purpose of the gospel of Jesus Christ is to restore, heal and change the Sixty into who they can become.

The symbolism of the Sixty is a reminder that God believes in powerful comebacks. Members of the Sixty include: Ammon, Aaron, Omner, Himni, Amulek, Zeezrom, Paul, Alma the Elder, and Alma the younger. We are all honorary members of the Sixty in one way or another due to our sins and due to our neglect of weighty matters. The symbolism of the Sixty reminds us that a little mercy travels such a great distance.

We have had a pool most of our life in Arizona, and have had a few scary near drowning experiences. Arizona pools are wonderful in the summer, but each year a number of children drown due to no pool fences or faulty pool gates. These events have made us extremely cautious in our approach to our pool.

I remember one Saturday when my two-year-old daughter Holland was nowhere to be found in the house. After looking for her for a time inside with no success, I assumed she must be playing out back. I went into the backyard, and the first thing I saw was the pool gate propped open. In our family, the number one safety rule is to never leave the self-closing gate propped open. This was crucial at the time as little Holland could not swim, but loved the water.

When I saw the open pool gate knowing Holland wasn't inside the house, my heart sank about two feet. I could feel the panic in nearly every cell of my body. I immediately started to pray as I ran for the pool gate. My prayer was not really a prayer as much as a begging plea saying, "Please, no, Heavenly Father, please, no." It was a plea begging for mercy. I got to the pool area and looked into the deep end, and there was nothing. I then scanned the shallow end and again, nothing. I was so grateful that mercy had been granted.

I closed the gate, returned to the house, and found my sweet little daughter playing in the basement. I felt like Lehi in his dream when he said, "I began to pray unto the Lord that he would have mercy on me, according to the multitude of his tender mercies" (1 Nephi 8:8). Truly, the pool experience felt like a multitude of tender mercies had been bestowed upon me.

The symbol of the Sixty will always be a reminder to me of the thrill of mercy. Elder Holland said,

"It underscores the thought I heard many years ago that surely the thing God enjoys most about being God is the thrill of being merciful, especially to those who don't expect it and often feel they don't deserve it." (Jeffrey R. Holland, "Laborers in the Vineyard," Ensign, April 2012.)

I love this poem written by Mary Lyman Henry, entitled "To Any Who Have Watched for a Son's Returning".

He watched his son gather all the goods that were his lot, anxious to be gone from tending flocks, the dullness of the fields.

He stood by the olive tree gate long after the caravan disappeared where the road climbs the hills on the far side of the valley, into infinity.

Through changing seasons, he spent the light in a great chair, facing the far country, and that speck of road on the horizon.

Mocking friends: "He will not come." Whispering servants: "The old man has lost his senses." A chiding son: "You should not have let him go." A grieving wife: "You need rest and sleep."

She covered his drooping shoulders, his callused knees, when east winds blew chill, until that day . . .
A form familiar, even at infinity, in shreds, alone, stumbling over pebbles.

"When he was a great way off, His father saw him, and had compassion, and ran, and fell on his neck, and kissed him." (Luke 15:20)

[Mary Lyman Henry, Ensign, March 1983, p. 63].

Let us remember what a loving Father in Heaven did for those who missed the first opportunity to serve and later enlisted to join Helaman's army. During the battle of Cumeni, we see the power of the righteous 2,060 stripling warriors: *"But behold, my little band of two thousand and sixty fought most desperately; yea, they were firm before the Lamanites, and did administer death unto all those who opposed them. And as the remainder of our army were about to give way before the Lamanites, behold, those two thousand and sixty were firm and undaunted. Yea, and they did obey and observe to perform every word of command with exactness; yea, and even according to their faith it was done unto them; and I did remember the words which they said unto me that their mothers had taught them. And now behold, it was these my sons, and those men who had been selected to convey the prisoners, to whom we owe this great victory; for it was they who did beat the Lamanites; therefore, they were driven back to the city of Manti" (Alma 57:19-22, emphasis added).*

When the battle of Cumeni was over, we see that the soldiers were again accounted for:

> *And it came to pass that there were two hundred, out of my two thousand and sixty, who had fainted because of the loss of blood; nevertheless, according to the goodness of God, and to our great astonishment, and also the joy of our whole army, there was not one soul of them who did perish; yea, and neither was there one soul among them who had not received many wounds. And now, their preservation was astonishing to our whole army, yea, that they should be spared while there was a thousand of our brethren who were slain. And we do justly ascribe it to the miraculous power of God, because of their exceeding faith*

in that which they had been taught to believe—that there was a just God, and whosoever did not doubt, that they should be preserved by his marvellous power. Now this was the faith of these of whom I have spoken; they are young, and their minds are firm, and they do put their trust in God continually" *(Alma 57:25-27, emphasis added).*

The Lord had taken the Sixty and filled them with exceeding faith, given them the strength to obey every command with exactness, and blessed them with an abundance of His mercy. The Sixty, although late to enlist, were blessed just as the other 2000 had been as they joined the greatest cause on earth. Those Sixty were given every blessing God had to offer someone who enlisted earlier. They may have been late to the battle, but they were supported by the hand of God in every aspect of their fight.

It is difficult not to think of Alma who was a sitting politician working for King Noah. Alma had been less active for a time. He had known that he should be engaged in God's work, but he had not been. Like the Sixty, he had a chance to join with all his heart, might, mind and strength, but he hadn't initially. To Alma's credit, despite being late, he enlisted. He heard the prophet Abinadi testify and the fire in his heart was rekindled again. He stood, he reenlisted, and he was never the same again. A loving God blessed him with strength as he made righteous choices and another stripling soldier of God was engaged. He never looked back after his second chance.

I work with a lady named Sally who was baptized just a few years ago. She is teaching in her ward primary and doing wonderfully trying to live the gospel principles. Sally is in her 40's. She has a 22-year-old son and a 16-year-old son. She came to BYU Education week recently and said, "This is amazing. This is inspiring. I am in awe. I am so impressed." After sitting through yet another class and being touched over and over again by gospel truths, Sally simply said, "I wish I would have had this fifteen years ago for my kids." I loved her insightful comments, but told Sally, "It's okay. The Lord brought it to you when He did." Sally is entitled to every possible blessing the gospel of Jesus Christ has to offer.

My thoughts were like Sally's; it would have been great, but it is never too late-- not for you, not for your kids, and not for your loved ones. The symbol of the Sixty reminds us again and again that with God, it is never too late. The thrill of mercy may strike in your life at any time. A merciful God will always be aware opportunities have been lost, but he will always create more. Our God would never have us dwell on the could-have's when we have so many will-have's yet to come. Sally is late, but she has arrived with life changing desires, dreams and hopes.

I was reminded again of miracles during a college football game in 2017. On a sunny Saturday afternoon, UCLA was playing Texas A&M. With 4:08 left in the third quarter, Texas A&M had just kicked a field goal to go up 44-10. Some of the sports networks occasionally post on their websites the statistical win probability. There was a point late in the 3rd quarter of the game where the UCLA Bruins statistically had a .1% chance of winning. This statistically means it was really impossible for UCLA to come back and win. Their chance at winning the game for all intents and purposes was over. The quarterback Josh Rosen said, "It got real bleak at a certain point- real, real bleak." Haven't we all felt that bleak feeling at some time in our lives when things are rough and we are spiritually losing?

UCLA then--metaphorically speaking-- came back from the dead. In an absolute reversal of fate, nearly everything went their way for the next seventeen minutes. They made critical stops, unexpected catches, their blocking improved, their defense played stronger, and they even barely blocked a field goal that would have put the game out of reach. When the final gun sounded, UCLA had scored 35 points in the last seventeen minutes to miraculously win the game. Josh Rosen said, "We were an inch away from losing that game probably 10 times."
(www.espn.com/video/clipTest?id=2056 9001). There is power in that statement.

In the game of life, we may be down, and others may think we have no chance to come back, but through the miracle of the Atonement of Jesus Christ, we can come back. We can turn defeat into victory, we can be successful, we can play better, we can defend better, we can be more protected, we can win, we can change the outcome, we can see miracles happen that turn things around. This is what the Sixty do; they win with Christ even when they may have been inches away from losing without Him. The Sixty echo the words of Paul who said, "But thanks be to God, which giveth us the victory through our Lord Jesus Christ (1 Corinthians 15:57).

President Gordon B. Hinckley shared this experience about Joseph F. Smith that is a powerful reminder of those who come to the kingdom, but come late:

> Joseph F. Smith was the son of Hyrum Smith, who was the brother of the Prophet Joseph and was martyred with him in Carthage. Joseph F. was born at Far West, Missouri, on November 13, 1838. He came out of Missouri as an

infant. As a lad not yet six years of age, he heard a knock on the window of his mother's home in Nauvoo. It was a man who had hurriedly ridden from Carthage and who told Sister Smith that her husband had been killed that afternoon.

When he was 9, he drove an ox team with his mother across the plains to this valley. At the age of 15 he was called on a mission to Hawaii. He made his way to San Francisco and there worked in a shingle mill to earn enough money to buy passage to the islands.

Hawaii was not a tourist center then. It was populated by the native Hawaiians, who were, for the most part, poor but generous with what they had. He learned to speak their language and to love them. While serving there he experienced a remarkable dream. I quote from his narrative concerning this. Said he:

"I was very much oppressed [when I was] on a mission. I was almost naked and entirely friendless, except [for] the friendship of a poor, benighted … people. I felt as if I was so debased in my condition of poverty, lack of intelligence and knowledge, just a boy, that I hardly dared look a … man in the face.

While in that condition I dreamed [one night] that I was on a journey, and I was impressed that I ought to hurry—hurry with all my might, for fear I might be too late. I rushed on my way as fast as I possibly could, and I was only conscious of having just a little bundle, a handkerchief with a small bundle wrapped in it. I did not realize … what it was, when I was hurrying as fast as I could; but finally I came to a wonderful mansion. … I thought I knew that was my destination. As I passed towards it, as fast as I could, I saw a notice [which read B-A-T-H], 'Bath.' I turned aside quickly and went into the bath and washed myself clean. I opened up this little bundle that I had, and there was [some] white, clean [clothing], a thing I had not seen for a long time, because the people I was with did not think very much of making things exceedingly clean. But my [clothing was] clean, and I put [it] on. Then I rushed to what appeared to be a great opening, or door. I knocked and the door opened, and the man who stood there was the Prophet Joseph Smith. He looked at me a little reprovingly, and the first words he said: 'Joseph, you are late.' Yet I took confidence and [replied]:'Yes, but I am clean—I am clean!' He clasped my hand and drew me in, then closed the great door. I felt his hand just as tangible as I ever felt the hand of man. I knew him, and when I entered I saw my father, and Brigham [Young] and Heber [C. Kimball], and Willard [Richards], and other good men that I had known, standing in a row. I looked as if it were across this valley, and it seemed to be filled with a vast multitude of people, but on the stage were all the people that I had known. My mother was there, and she sat with a child in her lap; and I could name over as many as I remember of their names, who sat there, who seemed to be among the chosen, among the exalted.'" (Gordon B. Hinckley "I am Clean" April 2007).

The true and lasting lesson of the Sixty is that they went to battle later, but most importantly, they went. The Sixty joined, they enlisted, they exercised faith, they participated, they testified, they acted, they obeyed, they embraced the gospel of Jesus Christ. They were absolutely clean because of the blood of Christ. The Sixty are the repentant "whose garments are white through the blood of the Lamb" (Ether 13:10).

We may not all enlist at the same time, but we all must enlist and be patient with those who enlist a little later. May we never penalize the latecomers. Like the Sixty Stripling Warriors, the late comers may be the very people who defend, support and sustain us when we need it the most. May we love them, invite them, pray for them, and show mercy to them as they, like us are truly a symbol of the Sixty. May the Sixty always be a reminder to us that spiritual cleanliness will always be more important than timeliness.

When my son Blake was about eight, we went to the desert one day to have a paintball gun encounter. It was going to be a great family day with a few friends. My sons and I and a few friends were all there having team paintball battles when Blake arrived. Blake came a little later than the rest of us as he had another commitment that conflicted. Immediately, when my wife dropped Blake off at the desert he was upset because someone was using "his" gun. He went on and on in his complaining and wouldn't stop. I warned Blake a few times that he was going to be sent home if he continued. He saw my wife drive away, so he was certain this was just a threat and would never happen. He never stopped with his attitude and complaining and so action needed to be taken.

I called my wife back and asked her to return to pick Blake up, as he wasn't yielding or relenting, making enjoyment of the activity difficult for any of us. When my wife showed back up, I threw young Blake over my shoulder and headed through the desert brush back to the car. When he saw the car and realized his paintball experience was over, his tune began to change. He went from angry and belligerent to crying and pleading. He begged me not to send him home. He tried every bit of reasoning he could think of. He said, "Dad, please just give me another chance." I told him that he had been given numerous warnings and numerous chances to stop, but he wouldn't stop. It was about a 90 second walk back to the car through the desert and his pleading went on for some time.

Finally, as we neared the car in a final desperate last plea, Blake said something that struck a chord in me that I will never forget, "Dad, please, please give me a second chance; Heavenly Father always gives second chances."

I have learned many lessons in my life, but the lesson I have learned most forcefully and most frequently is what Blake reminded me of that day. God always gives second chances. If you are one of the Sixty currently idly waiting in the marketplace, not yet enlisted, please remember that we believe in a God of second chances.

About the Author

As a young man, Jeffrey "Jeff" Erickson served a full-time mission in the Canada Halifax Mission. Jeff and his amazing wife, Christine, have six sons and one daughter and reside in Gilbert, Arizona.

Jeff has been a youth speaker at Especially For Youth (EFY) for many years. He has served faithfully in many capacities in the church including gospel doctrine instructor and bishop. He has a passion for writing and speaking about the gospel of Jesus Christ.

He is the recent author of "A Weekly Letter to Your Missionary." He is also the author of the first book in *"The Greater View Series"* called "The Fourth Nephite Effect."

Jeff is one of the co-founders of NSFC (Non-Sunday futbol club) Strikers. This two-year old soccer club is the first non-Sunday competitive soccer club in Arizona.

Made in the USA
San Bernardino, CA
02 February 2018